THE USBORNE BOOK OF AMAZING FEATS

Anita Ganeri

CONTENTS

Illustrated by Tony Gibson, Cathy Simpson, Guy Smith and Chris Shields

Designed by Tony Gibson

Consultants: Dr. John Becklake, Dr. David Billett, Shirley Bond, Rob Lovell, Dr. Anne Millard, Rosie Smith, Trudy Waters and Marc Woodward

SCHOLASTIC INC.
New York Toronto London Auckland Sydney

Against the odds

Earthquake babies

In September 1985, a huge earthquake hit Mexico City, killing over 2,000 people. Among many other buildings, the city's maternity hospital was flattened by the earthquake. Deep under the rubble, however, rescue workers found over 50 new-born babies. They were covered with dirt and grime, but were still alive.

Avalanche alert

Avalanches are huge slides of snow. Millions of tons of snow can fall at speeds of up to 250mph (400kph) down a mountain. Avalanches kill about 150 people a year. In 1900, a Swiss forestry worker was hurled through the air by an avalanche. He landed in thick snow, alive but badly shocked, some 2,200ft (670m) further down the mountain.

Tornado travel

In May 1986, a group of 12 schoolchildren in China were sucked up by a tornado. The tornado carried them 12 miles (20km) and dropped them among some sand dunes. All the children escaped completely unharmed.

Cast adrift

In 1789, the crew of the *HMS Bounty* mutinied. They cast the captain, William Bligh, and 18 sailors loyal to him, adrift in the middle of the Pacific Ocean in a small, open boat. In an amazing feat of survival and seamanship, Bligh managed to sail the 23ft (7m) long boat safely to the island of Timor some 4,100 miles (6,700 km) away. The ordeal lasted 43 days.

In a hole

The Scottish climber, David Hamilton, survived for three days at the bottom of a deep hole in the snow near the summit of Mount Blanc in France. Rescuers could not reach him any sooner because of a terrible storm raging on the mountain. He put his survival down to his sense of humor.

Amazing But True

In a bombing raid over Germany in March 1944, Flight Sergeant Nicholas Alkemade's plane was hit by a shell and caught fire. Alkemade jumped from the plane, 18,000ft (5,485m) off the ground, without using a parachute. He landed unhurt and still conscious, despite having travelled through the air as fast as an express train. His fall was broken by springy tree branches and drifts of deep snow.

Jungle adventure

In 1982, an American, Eric Hansen, survived for four months in the jungle of Borneo. He was the first foreigner ever to do this. Helped by native guides, he travelled by dug-out canoe and on foot. He lived on whatever he could shoot or catch. This included monkeys, bats, boa constrictors, fruit and bee larvae.

Going underground

In 1964, a group of cavers were trapped by floods 2,600ft (792m) down in the Berger Cave, France. All they could do was wait for the water to go down. One of the biggest dangers they faced was getting too cold. So, for two whole days and nights, they slept for just an hour at a time, getting up in between to run and jump in place.

DID YOU KNOW?

In 1942, a sailor, Poon Lim, survived for 133 days alone on a raft in the middle of the Atlantic Ocean after his ship was sunk. He had enough provisions to last for the first 50 days. For the next 83 days he lived on raw fish, seagull meat and rainwater. He caught the fish with a nail which he shaped into a hook with his teeth. He was rescued by a fishing boat.

Lucky escape

In May 1902, Mount Pelée, on the Caribbean island of Martinique, erupted with a mighty bang. The nearby city of St. Pierre was almost completely destroyed. Only three members of its population of 28,000 survived. One was a prisoner, called August Cyparis. He had been serving his sentence in the stone jail – the only building in the whole city to survive the eruption.

Fighting the ice

In 1914, the explorer, Ernest Shackleton, set sail to explore Antarctica. In the Weddell Sea, however, his ship, *Endurance,* was crushed by the ice and sank. The crew drifted on icebergs, then in boats, to a windswept island. Then Shackleton and five others set sail again in a small, open boat. They sailed 800 miles (1,280km) over the world's stormiest seas to South Georgia to get help. Thanks to them, every member of Shackleton's crew was saved.

Incredible journeys

Around Africa

In about 600BC, Pharaoh Necho II of Egypt sent an expedition to sail around Africa. This had never been tried before. The sailors set out in flimsy boats with no cabins. They returned two years later, having completed the round trip of 16,000 miles (25,750km). Portuguese explorers were the next to attempt this feat – over 2,000 years later.

Amazon adventure

In 1542, Francisco de Orellana became the first European to cross South America. He travelled most of the way along the Amazon River. The journey took 17 months. On the way, he ran out of food and had to eat leather saddles and belts, together with snakes and toads. He was attacked by crocodiles, and lost an eye in a fight with local tribesmen.

Saharan crossing

In the 1820s, the Geographical Society of Paris offered a large prize to the first European to cross the Sahara Desert. But no one believed the French explorer, René Caillié, when he said he had done it. The 1,000 mile (1,610km) journey took him just over a year. He was later given his prize.

Travelling ways

Between 1325-53, the Moroccan, Ibn Battuta, travelled 75,000 miles (120,000km). He went as far east as China, as far north as Russia and crossed the Sahara Desert. He travelled on foot or by camel and had no maps to guide him. Instead, he navigated by the Sun and the stars. He never took the same route twice.

DID YOU KNOW?

About 3,000 years ago, Polynesian sailors explored a huge area of the Pacific Ocean. They travelled in canoes with no maps or compasses to guide them. Instead, they used wave patterns. They could read these so accurately that they could pinpoint the position of an island 100 miles (160km) away.

Across Africa

David Livingstone first went to Africa in 1840. In 1851, he crossed the Kalahari Desert and discovered the Zambezi River. Between 1852-56, he became the first European to travel across Africa. He covered vast distances on foot, on ox-back or by dug-out canoe.

Great explorers

Date	Explorer	Feat
1271-95	Marco Polo	Travelled from Italy to China.
1499-1501	Amerigo Vespucci	Explored South American coast.
1519-22	Ferdinand Magellan	First expedition to sail around the world.
1772-3	James Cook	Discovered Antarctica.
1803-4	Meriwether Lewis/ William Clark	First expedition to cross North American continent.
1874	H. M. Stanley	Discovered source of River Nile.
1909	Robert Peary	Claimed to be first at North Pole.
1970-4	David Kunst	First (verified) walk round world.
1986-9	Robert Swann	First to walk to both Poles.

Race for the Pole

On 14 December 1911, the Norwegian explorer, Roald Amundsen, and his four companions became the first people to reach the South Pole. Despite freezing cold, blizzards and frostbite, they made the round trip of 1,860 miles (2,995km) in just 99 days.

Saved by her skirts

In 1893, the intrepid English explorer, Mary Kingsley, made her first journey to Africa. Even in the jungle, she still wore long skirts, as she had at home. These skirts saved her life when she fell into a deep pit, ringed with sharp spikes. Her skirts caught on the spikes and her companions were able to pull her out safely.

Over Australia

The first people to cross Australia from south to north had never been exploring before. Robert Burke and William Wills made the 1,488 mile (2,400km) journey in 1861. They survived by eating their camels when they ran out of food. Sadly, both men died on the return journey.

Confused Columbus

One of the greatest feats of exploration was achieved by mistake. When Christopher Columbus discovered the new continent of America in 1492, he was sure he had landed in Asia. No one could ever persuade him he was wrong.

Amazing But True

In 1975, an English clergyman, Geoffrey Howard, crossed the Sahara Desert from north to south. For the whole of the 1,200 mile (1,930km) journey he pushed a wheelbarrow full of supplies. His journey took three months.

Climbing high

On top of the world

The first people to stand on the summit of Mount Everest, the world's highest mountain, were Edmund Hillary and Sherpa Tenzing Norgay on 29 May, 1953. Ten previous expeditions had failed to reach the top. Over 130 climbers have now reached Everest's summit. Many more have died on the way.

Everest firsts

Record	Climbers
First to summit (1953)	Tenzing/Hillary
Most ascents (6)	Ang Rita Sherpa
First solo climb (1980)	Reinhold Messner
Without oxygen (1978)	Reinhold Messner and Peter Habeler
First woman to summit (1975)	Junko Tabei
Oldest to summit (55 yrs)	Dick Bass

DID YOU KNOW?

The Matterhorn in Switzerland is 14,668ft (4,477m) high, with steep sides all the way around. The first woman to climb it was Lucy Walker in 1871. For climbing, she wore a full-skirted dress and a veiled hat. The only food she took along with her was sponge cake and champagne.

Mountain hound

In 1875, a beagle, called Tschingel, climbed Mont Blanc, the highest mountain in the Alps. This was not her only climbing feat. Between 1868-1876 she climbed 53 of the most difficult mountains in the Alps.

Kenyan adventure

Mount Kenya is 17,057ft (5,199m) high, the second highest peak in Africa. In 1899, Sir Halford Mackinder became the first person to reach its summit, despite being attacked on the way by rhinos, and tribesmen armed with poisoned arrows.

Hold tight

In 1882, an Irish vicar, William Green, and his two guides climbed to within 300ft (60m) of the summit of Mount Cook in New Zealand. Terrible weather and avalanches forced them to turn back.

Before they could reach the bottom, darkness fell. They spent the night perched on a tiny 2ft (60cm) wide ledge. They sang songs to keep awake, so that they would not fall off.

Amazing But True

The fastest descent of Everest was made by Erhard Loretan and Jean Troillet in 1986. They slid down 8,000ft (2,438m) on their bottoms, with just ice axes as brakes. The slide took 3.5 hours.

Super climber

Out of all the mountains in the world, only 14 are higher than 26,250ft (8,000m). From 1970 to 1986, the Italian climber, Reinhold Messner, climbed them all. He was the first person ever to achieve this feat.

Eating out

In 1989, nine Australian climbers climbed to the top of Mount Huascaran in Peru...to have their dinner! They carried a table, chairs, wine and a three course meal to the summit, 22,205ft (6,768m) up. There they changed into dinner suits and ball gowns and sat down to eat. The wine, unfortunately, had frozen solid in its bottle.

Everest by canoe

In 1976, two British canoeists, Mike Jones and Mike Hopkinson, canoed down the Dudh Kosi River in Nepal. The river starts at a height of 17,500ft (5,334m) on an icy lake high up on the Khumbu Glacier. The very dangerous Everest icefall looms above it, so there is a constant risk of snow slides and avalanches.

Getting down

At 22,835ft (6,960m), Mount Aconcagua in Argentina is the highest mountain in North or South America. In the early 1980s, two French climbers, Boivin and Marchal, came down the mountain not by foot, but by hang-glider. They landed some 10,000ft (3,048m) below the summit, having soared freely for 20 minutes.

First ascent of each continent's highest peak

Peak	Location	Climber(s)	Year
Elbrus	USSR (Europe)	Gardiner	1874
Kilimanjaro	Tanzania (Africa)	Meyer/Purtscheller	1889
Cook	New Zealand (Australasia)	Fyfe/Graham/Clarke	1894
Aconcagua	Argentina (South America)	Zurbriggen	1897
McKinley	Alaska (North America)	Karstens/Stuck/Harper/Tatum	1913
Everest	Tibet/Nepal (Asia)	Hillary/Tenzing	1953
Vinson Massif	Antarctica	Clinch	1966

Living dangerously

Walking on fire

Firewalking is part of religious ceremonies in many parts of the world. In Fiji, priests walk barefoot across a deep pit filled with red-hot stones. Amazingly, even the soles of their feet do not get burned. In some Aboriginal tribes in Australia, boys have to walk through fire to make them fearless.

Freezing flight

Armando Soccaras Ramirez made a terrifying 5,600 mile (9,010km) journey in 1969. He flew from Cuba to Spain in the wheel compartment underneath a plane. On the eight-hour flight, he survived temperatures as low as −40°F (−40°C) and was taken up to 29,000ft (8,800m).

Flying like a bird

For centuries, people have tried to fly like birds. In 1931, an American, Clem Sohn, jumped out of a plane 10,000ft (3,000m) above the ground. He had cloth wings stretched between his arms, legs and body. He glided down to a height of about 1,000ft (300m) before he plummeted to his death.

Amazing But True

In 1835, an Indian fakir was locked into a chest and buried under the ground. The chest was dug up 40 days later and the fakir emerged alive and well. He seemed to survive by lowering his heartbeat and breathing rate to save energy. This is exactly what animals do when they hibernate in the winter.

Bridge jumping

Members of the Dangerous Sports Club in Oxford, England, do dangerous things for fun. In 1982, one of the members threw himself off the Royal Gorge Bridge in Colorado. The bridge is 1,030ft (320m) above the Arkansas River, higher than the Eiffel Tower in Paris. He survived, although his only link with the bridge was an elastic rope tied around his ankles.

Wing walking

In 1980, Jaromir Wagner of Czechoslovakia set off from Scotland to fly across the Atlantic Ocean. However, he did not sit inside the aircraft. He travelled the whole way standing on top of its wings.

The men of the Pentecost Islands in the South Pacific have a death-defying way of proving their courage. They dive from a bamboo tower some 90ft (27.5m) high. This is like diving from a seven-story building. Long vines tied around their ankles allow them to swing just above the ground. If the vines snap, though, the divers crash to certain death.

Risky records

Category	Record
Longest stay underwater (holding breath)	13 mins, 42.5 secs
Highest stilts used in stiltwalking	40ft 6.5in (12.36m)
Longest time spent buried alive	141 days
Longest time spent on a tightrope	185 days
Longest descent by rappelling	3,250ft (990m)

Worst great escape

In 1975, 75 Mexican convicts began digging a tunnel to take them out of prison. Six months later their work was finished. Sadly, the tunnel came up right inside a courtroom. As each convict crawled out of the tunnel, the judge sent him straight back to prison.

Skyscraper stroll

In 1974, Philippe Petit of France was arrested on an extraordinary trespassing charge. He had been walking along a tightrope stretched between the two towers of the World Trade Center in New York. The rope was stretched 1,350ft (411m) above the ground. Before his arrest he had already crossed it seven times.

Human fly

In 1920, an American, George Gibson Polley, climbed halfway up the Woolworth building in New York without using ropes. He had reached the 30th floor of the 729ft (241m) tower when he was arrested for climbing without first getting permission.

Over a barrel

In 1901, a teacher, Anna Edson Taylor, became the first person to ride over Niagara Falls in a barrel. She was badly shaken after the 160ft (54m) drop, but survived her ordeal intact.

Risky business

The amazing Blondin

In 1859, the Frenchman, Blondin, walked across Niagara Falls on a tightrope. The rope was stretched 160ft (50m) above the rushing waters. A few months later, Blondin crossed with his business manager on his back. On one crossing, he took a small gas stove with him. Halfway across, he stopped, and cooked and ate an omelette!

Sword swallowing

Most people would injure themselves if they tried swallowing a sword. Some experts, though, can swallow sharp blades as long as a person's arm. They practice for years to make the sword go safely down the throat and into the stomach.

Eating fire

Fire eaters have been entertaining people since the time of the Ancient Greeks. Today, the record for fire eating is 22,888 torches in two hours. Fire eaters often seem to swallow the fire, then blow it out of their mouths again, sending flames up to 30ft (10m) long shooting out.

DID YOU KNOW?

Harry Houdini was one of the greatest escape artists there has ever been. He was famous for his underwater escapes from heavy, padlocked chests, even when he was handcuffed and bound with chains. Another of his tricks was swallowing some needles and a piece of thread. Then he would pull the thread out again with all the needles neatly threaded on.

Taming lions

Lion taming is one of the most dangerous circus acts. Over 20 lion tamers have been fatally injured in the last 90 years. One of the most skillful lion tamers was Clyde Raymond Beatty. A lion tamer for 40 years, he once handled 40 lions and tigers at a time.

Bird's nesters

The Chinese delicacy, bird's-nest soup, is made from the nests of swiftlets, who live deep inside caves. The nests are so valuable that collectors risk their lives to get them. In Thailand, they climb up rickety bamboo scaffolds over 300ft (90m) high or cling to vines tied to giant stalactites inside the caves.

Free falling

Film stuntmen take risks for a living. In 1979, a stuntman called Dar Robinson jumped 1,170ft (360m) from the CN Tower in Toronto, Canada. He opened his parachute seconds before he hit the ground, having timed the stunt to perfection. He had worked out that he had just 10 seconds to fall, open his parachute and land safely.

Chinese magic

Chung Ling Soo was a famous magician of the early 1900s. His most daring trick was to be shot at with fake bullets which he caught on a china plate, like the one below, held in front of him. In 1918, a trick went wrong. One of the trick guns was faulty. It fired real bullets which killed him.

Amazing But True

In 1929, Hugo Zacchini was shot 135ft (40m) from the mouth of a cannon. He travelled at 80mph (130kph), the speed of a fast car. Five years later, Hugo and his brother were shot at the same time from a cannon at a circus in New York. Hugo's act was carried on by his son and granddaughter. Both of them became human cannonballs.

High divers

Professional divers in Acapulco, Mexico, regularly dive from a height of 87.5ft (26.7m) to earn their living. They dive head-first from a huge cliff called La Quebrada into the sea below. The water here is only 12ft (3.5m) deep.

Bungled burglary

Some risks are not worth taking. In 1933, a burglar in Paris went to rob a house, disguised in a suit of armor. The sound of the clanking armor soon woke the house owner up. He knocked the burglar over and called the police. To make matters worse, the fall badly dented the burglar's armor. He was stuck inside it for a further 24 hours.

Cycle jumping

Evel Knievel became famous for long-jumping over a line of buses, on a motorcycle. In 1974 he tried, and failed, to shoot across Snake River Canyon in the USA on a steam-powered motor-cycle. The Canyon is 1,600ft (485m) wide, equivalent to a line of 120 buses. By 1975, Evel Knievel's stunts had cost him 400 broken bones.

11

All at sea

Shipwreck survivor

In 1953, Alain Bombard set out from the Canary Islands in a small rubber boat to cross the Atlantic Ocean. He wanted to test out his theory that shipwrecked people could survive for days at sea. He lived on 1.5 pints (0.8 liters) of seawater a day and tiny sea plants. He reached the West Indies 65 days later, having travelled 2,750 miles (4,400km). He was 56lb (25kg) thinner, but had proved his point.

Octopus thief

Octopuses are normally shy creatures and do not attack people. In 1960, though, an octopus attacked a fisherman in South Africa. After a struggle, the man got free, but the nimble octopus had managed to steal his gold watch from him.

Deep diving

In January 1960, the bathyscaphe, *Trieste*, dived 35,813ft (10,916m) down into the Marianas Trench in the Pacific Ocean. At this depth, the pressure of the water is equivalent to two cars balanced on your thumbnail. The two-man crew travelled in a steel chamber with walls 5in (13cm) thick, to keep them from being crushed.

World beater

In 1519, Ferdinand Magellan set out from Spain with five ships and 260 men to sail around the world. The sailors suffered very badly on the voyage. When food was low, they had to eat grilled strips of leather. Magellan himself was killed. Three years later, the successful expedition returned, reduced to one ship.

Voyaging Vikings

The Vikings may have discovered America 507 years before Columbus. According to ancient Norse writings, Leif the Lucky reached America in AD985. The Vikings crossed the Atlantic in light, wooden longboats. They navigated by the Sun, stars and the movements of sea birds.

Amazing But True

Great white sharks have a terrible reputation for eating people, though very many of these stories are untrue. In 1829, however, fishermen caught a 22ft (6.7m) shark off the coast of France. In its stomach they found the body of a headless man, in a complete suit of armor!

Sailing round the world

Record	Captain and ship	Dates
Earliest	Juan Sebastian del Cano *Vittoria* expedition	1519-1522
First solo	Joshua Slocum *Spray*	1895-1898
First non-stop solo	Robin Knox Johnston *Suhaili*	1968-1969
First underwater	Edward L. Beach *Triton* (submarine)	February to May 1960
Most non-stop solos	John Sanders *Parry Endeavour*	1986-1988 3 times
First motorboat	Albert Gowen *Speejacks*	1921-1922

Raft adventure

In 1947, Thor Heyerdahl set out to prove that the Incas of Peru had sailed to the Pacific Islands 1,500 years ago, on light, wooden rafts. Heyerdahl built his own raft, called *Kon-tiki*. He and his crew lived on rainwater and flying fish, as the Incas had done. They reached the Pacific island of Raroia four months later.

Row the boat

In August 1982, Peter Bird set off on an amazing journey to row solo across the Pacific Ocean. His boat, called *Hele-on-Britannia,* was just 32ft (9.75m) long, not much longer than a canoe. He reached the Great Barrier Reef in Australia in June 1983. He had rowed for 294 days and had covered 9,000 miles (14,480km).

Ice crossing

In 1958, the US nuclear submarine, *Nautilus,* became the first vessel ever to cross the Arctic Ocean. It sailed for a distance of 1,830 miles (2,945km) under the ice covering the ocean.

DID YOU KNOW?

The first person to sail solo around the world could not swim. In 1895, Captain Joshua Slocum set out from Boston in an old oyster boat, called *Spray*. He returned three years later, after a journey of some 46,000 miles (74,000km). Slocum had to give lectures on the way to finance his trip. In 1909, he set out on another great adventure. Neither he nor *Spray* were ever seen again.

Space and beyond

Animal orbit

The first living creature to go into space was a dog, called Laika. She was launched in the Soviet Sputnik 2 spacecraft in November 1957, to see how space would affect living things. Laika died in space when her oxygen supply ran out.

First in space

On 12 April 1961, the Soviet cosmonaut, Yuri Gagarin, became the first man ever in space. He circled the Earth once in his spacecraft, Vostok 1, at a speed of 17,560mph (28,260kph). The journey lasted just over 89 minutes.

Seeing the dark side

As the Moon travels around the Earth, only one side of it is ever visible. In 1959, the Soviet Luna 3 spacecraft flew behind the Moon and took photographs of the dark side. This was the first time it had ever been seen.

DID YOU KNOW?

In 1971, Alan Shephard, the commander of Apollo 14, hit the first ever golf shot on the Moon. The Moon has much lower gravity than Earth. The energy needed to hit a 300yd (274m) shot on Earth, would send the ball 1 mile (1.6km) on the Moon.

Man on the Moon

On 21 July 1969, the American astronaut, Neil Armstrong, became the first person to step onto the Moon. By 1972, 12 astronauts had landed on the Moon. They brought back over 840lb (380kg) of moon rock and dust, worth thousands of times its weight in gold. The rock was at least 3,000 million years old.

Missions to the Moon

Spacecraft	Dates	Achievement
Apollo 11 (USA)	July 1969	Landed the first man on the Moon.
Apollo 12 (USA)	November 1969	Stayed on the Moon for 32 hours.
Apollo 13 (USA)	April 1970	Spacecraft exploded. Astronauts returned to Earth.
Apollo 14 (USA)	Jan-Feb 1971	Explored highland area of the Moon.
Apollo 15 (USA)	July-Aug 1971	Crew explored the Moon in a car, called a Lunar Rover.
Apollo 16 (USA)	April 1972	The Lunar Rover set a speed record for the Moon, at 11.2mph (18kph).

Unmanned planetary probes

Probe	Date launched	Achievement
Mariner 2 (USA)	August 1962	First fly-by of Venus.
Mariner 4 (USA)	November 1964	First fly-by of Mars.
Pioneer 10 (USA)	March 1972	First fly-by of Jupiter.
Pioneer 11 (USA)	April 1973	First fly-by of Saturn.
Mariner 10 (USA)	November 1973	First TV pictures of Venus and Mercury.
Venera 13 (USSR)	October 1981	First soil analysis of the surface of Venus.

Amazing But True

Many people claim to have seen UFOs (Unidentified Flying Objects). In 1973, two men in the USA claimed they had been taken aboard a UFO by three aliens with no eyes. They were kept for 20 minutes while the aliens took photographs of them.

Space marathon

Vladimir Titov and Musa Manarov began a record-breaking spaceflight on 21 December 1987. They returned to Earth on 21 December 1988, having spent a year aboard their Mir space station.

Seeing stars

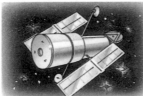

The Hubble space telescope was launched from the American Space Shuttle in April 1990. It is now orbiting the Earth, 300 miles (480km) above the ground. The telescope will be able to see space objects seven times further away or 50 times fainter than anything that is now visible.

Finding Pluto

Pluto is the smallest planet in our Solar System, five times smaller than the Moon. It was discovered in 1930, by an American astronomer, Clyde Tombaugh. It was the first planet to be discovered since Neptune in the 1800s and Uranus in 1781. The other six planets were discovered at the time of the Ancient Greeks, about 2,000 years ago.

Far, far away

Pioneer 10 was launched in 1972. By 1989 the probe passed Pluto and became the first man-made object to leave our Solar System. It carries a metal plaque with messages for any aliens who might intercept it. The plaque shows human beings, and the Earth's position in space.

On the move

Ocean rowing

It took 4,000 people to row the giant warship, *Tessarakonteres*. This huge ship was built for the Egyptian king, Ptolemy IV, in about 210BC. The ship was longer than a soccer field. Each oar was 57ft (17.5m) long and was pulled by eight men.

Driving marathon

In 1989, Mohammed Salauddin and his wife set out from Delhi, India, to drive right around the world. They completed the journey of 25,187 miles(40,534km) in 69 days, 19 hours and 5 minutes. They drove through six continents and a total of 25 countries.

Alpine elephants

In about 218BC, the Carthaginian general, Hannibal, set out to invade Italy and fight the Romans. To surprise the enemy, he performed an amazing military feat. He crossed the Alps in winter, with not only his huge army but also 37 elephants in tow.

Hover power

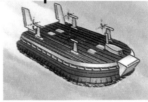

In the 1950s, Christopher Cockerell had the idea of using a vacuum cleaner to make boats go faster. He attached the cleaner to a boat and put its motor in reverse, so that it blew air under the boat. The result of his tests was the ancestor of the modern hovercraft above.

DID YOU KNOW?

When escalators were introduced in Britain in 1911, no one wanted to use them. A man known as Bumper Harris was employed to persuade them otherwise. It was his job to ride up and down on the escalator in Earl's Court station, London, to show people how safe it was.

Flying solo

In May 1927, the American pilot, Charles Lindbergh, became the first person to fly solo across the Atlantic. In his plane, the *Spirit of St Louis,* he covered the 3,600miles (5,790km) from London to New York in just over 33.5 hours. Today, the Concorde can make this journey in less than three hours.

Transport firsts

Ships' sails	3500BC
Airship	1852
Underground train	1863
Traffic lights	1868
Gas-driven car	1885
Car licence plates	1893
Powered flight	1903
Helicopter	1936

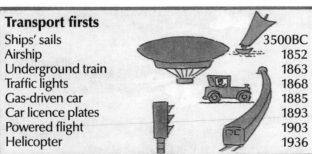

Hot-air animals

In November 1783, the French Montgolfier brothers became the first men ever to fly in a hot-air balloon. But they were not the first living things to travel by air. This honor was shared by a duck, a sheep and a cockerel. The brothers sent them up two months before their own flight, to see how well they survived. The animals landed, quite safely, after eight minutes in the air.

Cramped conditions

In 1986, two Americans, Dick Rutan and Jeana Yeager, became the first people to fly round the world without stopping to refuel their aircraft. The plane, *Voyager*, had been specially designed to carry over 3.3 tons of fuel. During the nine-day flight, each of the pilots lived in a space not much bigger than an average-sized bathtub.

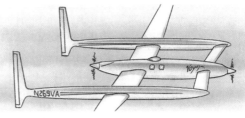

Worst tourist

In 1977, Nicholas Scotti tried to fly from San Francisco, USA, to Italy to visit relations. On the way, the plane stopped in New York. Mr Scotti spent two happy days there, convinced that he was in Rome.

Amazing But True

In 1769, a French army officer, Nicholas Cugnot, had the first known motor accident. He had invented a three-wheeled vehicle, powered by steam. Although the car only reached 2.25mph (3.6kph), Cugnot crashed into a wall minutes after starting. The huge boiler that powered the car made it impossible to steer.

Built for speed

Vehicle	Name	Speed
Passenger aircraft	Concorde	1,446mph/2,333kph
Flying boat	Martin XP6M-1 Seamaster	644mph/1,040kph
Car	Thrust 2	631mph/1,019kph
Submarine	Alfa-Class	48.2mph/77.8kph
Train	TGV (*Train à grande vitesse*)	319mph/515kph
Steam train	Mallard	125mph/202kph

Sporting moments

Unlimited overs

In 1939, the longest test cricket match was played in Durban, South Africa, between South Africa and England. The match lasted for 11 days and the players were on the field for just over 43 hours. Between them they bowled 5,070 balls and scored 1,981 runs. The match was finally called off because the England team's ship was due to leave for home.

It's a goal!

In a Scottish Cup soccer match in 1885, John Petrie scored a record 13 goals for his team, Arbroath, against Bon Accord. The final score was Arbroath 36, Bon Accord 0. The Arbroath goalkeeper did not touch the ball once.

Game, set and match

In a tennis match in 1983, Bill Scanlon of the USA beat Marcos Hocevar of Brazil 6-2, 6-0. He won the final set without losing a single point. This is the only example of a "golden set" known in professional tennis.

Amazing But True

A woman who played in a golf tournament in the USA in 1912, took 166 shots and two hours to get her ball into one hole. Her first shot landed in the river. She got into a boat and finally managed to hit the ball out of the water. Then she had to play through a wood. Most players reached the hole in just four shots.

In a good cause

On 25 May 1986, some 20 million runners took part in "Sport Aid" to raise money for charity. Races were run in 277 cities in 78 countries worldwide. The event raised an incredible $107 million.

Violin on skates

A Belgian musician, Joseph Merlin, is thought to have made the first pair of roller skates in 1760. He had been invited to a ball and wanted to make an impression on the other guests. He skated in to the ballroom, playing a violin. Unfortunately, he could not stop and crashed into a mirror.

High speed sport	
Fastest	**Speed in kph/mph**
Race horse	69.62/43.25
Cricket ball bowled	160.45/99.68
Skier	223.74/139
Water skier	230.26/143.06
Squash serve	232.7/144.5
Cyclist	245/152
Tennis serve	263/163

We are the champions

Category	Name	Event	Age
Youngest (world)	Gertrude Ederle (USA)	swimming	12 years, 298 days
Oldest (world)	Gerhard Weidner (Ger)	walking	41 years, 71 days
Youngest (Olympic)	Barbara Jones (USA)	sprinting	15 years, 123 days
Oldest (Olympic)	Patrick McDonald (USA)	discus throwing	42 years, 26 days

Marathon message

The modern marathon race was inspired by a Greek messenger, Pheidippides.

In 490BC, the Athenian army beat the Persians in battle at Marathon. Pheidippides was sent back to Athens with the good news. He ran the 22 miles (35km) non-stop, delivered his message, then died of heat exhaustion. Modern marathons are just over 26 miles (42km).

DID YOU KNOW?

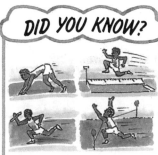

On 25 May 1935, the American athlete, Jesse Owens, set six world records in just 45 minutes. At the 1936 Berlin Olympics, Owens won four gold medals, in the 100m and 200m sprints, the long jump and the 4x100m relay.

Knock out!

In 1946 the boxer, Ralph Walton, was knocked out after just 10.5 seconds of his match with Al Couture. Walton was caught off guard as he adjusted his gum shield. The longest boxing match lasted over 7 hours in 1893. It was eventually declared a draw, because the boxers were too tired to carry on.

Tough going

The Paris-Dakar rally is the hardest motor race of all. Competitors have to drive nearly 6,820 miles (11,000 km) from Paris to Spain, then across the Sahara Desert to Dakar in Senegal. They face hazards such as 60 ft (18m) high sand dunes, thick sandstorms and scorching heat. The rally was first held in 1978.

Science and technology

Going metric

The metric system is used in many countries all over the world. It was invented about 200 years ago by a group of French scientists. It was based on a unit of length called the meter. This was calculated by dividing the distance between the Equator and the North Pole, through Paris, by 10 million.

Computers and calculators

Date	Machine
c.3,000BC	Abacus
1622	Slide rule
1642	First adding machine
1834	First digital computer (designed, but not built)
1945	First fully electronic calculator (ENIAC)
1948	First proper computer
1969	Microprocessor
1971	Pocket calculator
1975	First home computer

DID YOU KNOW?

The number system we use today was invented by Hindu mathematicians in India about 1,500 years ago. It was brought to Europe about 900 years ago, by Arab traders. The system quickly replaced Roman numerals which had been used for over a thousand years.

Laser power

A laser beam is a beam of very bright light, powerful enough to cut through metal. Lasers are also used in eye surgery to mend detached retinas and remove cataracts to restore sight. They can also remove tumors from the brain and spinal cord, which doctors could not otherwise reach.

High-speed printer

The world's fastest printer is a system made by an American company. It could print out the whole of this book in just over a second. This is some 3,300 times faster than the fastest typist in the world.

Super silicon

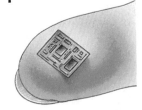

Silicon chips, which are also called microchips, form the "brains" of a computer. They can do calculations and store information. Amazingly, silicon chips are only about the size of a fingernail. Yet, in 1988, a Japanese company made a chip that could store the entire contents of a 160-page book on its surface.

Human or computer?

In 1983, a computer invented a new way of making electronic circuits, all by itself. It also decided that it was, in fact, a person. An American scientist had left the computer working every night to see if it could come up with anything by itself, or if it needed to be told exactly what to do.

Seeing things

The world's most powerful microscope was invented in 1981 by research scientists in Switzerland. It can magnify objects 100 million times. If the period at the end of this sentence was magnified by this much, it would be an incredible 62 miles (100km) wide.

Amazing But True

The most powerful computer in the world has a memory capable of storing 256 million 8-letter words at a time. This supercomputer is the CRAY-2, built by Cray Research Inc, USA.

Glass talk

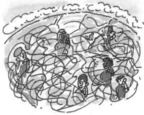

A fiber optic cable, made of strands of glass each the width of a human hair, can carry thousands of telephone calls. These cables use light to carry messages. In 1966, two scientists tried using them instead of copper cables to carry telephone calls. There are now thousands of miles of fiber optic cables all over the world.

Blood exchange

A French doctor carried out the first ever blood transfusion in 1667. It was a very tricky operation in which a young man was given 2 pints (1.1 liters) of blood … from a sheep. In 1818, an English doctor, James Blundell, transferred blood from one person to another, with a syringe. This was the first transfusion from person to person.

Medical milestones

Date	Discovery/First
1796	Smallpox vaccine
1816	Stethoscope
1844	Anesthetics
1853	Hypodermic syringe
1863	Clinical thermometer
1895	X-rays
1897	Synthetic aspirin
1960	Measles vaccine
1967	Heart transplant

Inventions and discoveries

Amazing feet

Amazonian Indians had been making rubber boots for some 650 years before Wellington boots were first made in 1851. The Indians dipped their legs and feet in the sticky sap of rubber trees. When the sap hardened, it formed a tough skin which provided them with protection from thorns and insect bites.

Zipped up

The zip fastener was invented in 1893 by an American, Whitcomb L. Judson. It was not a great success at first as the teeth kept springing apart or sticking. The design was improved in 1913. Over 250,000 miles (400,000km) of zips are now made each year. This is enough to reach the Moon.

Sucking and blowing

The first vacuum cleaner blew, instead of sucking. First shown in 1901, it covered the audience with dust. One of the onlookers, Hubert Booth, reversed the idea and invented the first suction cleaner. It was so big, it had to be pulled along by a horse.

Amazing But True

In 1903, Andrew Jackson invented a pair of spectacles for chickens. They were not to help the chickens' eyesight but to protect their eyes from being pecked.

Leonardo's genius

Leonardo da Vinci, the Italian artist and inventor, drew up plans for making a car, an aircraft and a helicopter in the 15th century, long before they were invented. The first helicopter was not made until 1936, over 400 years after Leonardo's death.

Plant plastic

Since they were first made in 1862, plastics have changed the world. The first man-made plastic was called bakelite. Discovered in 1909 by a Belgian scientist, L. Baekeland, it was made from coal tar gas and a gas called formaldehyde. The first ever cellophane was made in 1912.

Communications inventions

Object	Date	Inventor
Printing press	c.1450	Johannes Gutenberg
Telephone	1876	Alexander Graham Bell
Gramophone record	1891	Emile Berliner
Television (first demonstration)	1925	John Logie Baird
Transistor radio	1954	Regency Company
Cassette recorder	1963	Philips Company
Compact disc	1982	Philips and Sony

Famous inventions

Object	Date	Inventor/Where first used
Scissors	c.1,000BC	Europe and Asia
Paper	c. AD100	China
Fizzy drinks	1772	Joseph Priestly (GB)
Battery	1800	Alessandro Volta (Italy)
Safety pin	1849	W. Hunt (USA)
Can opener	1855	Mr Yates (GB)
Typewriter	1874	Christopher Sholes (USA)
Contact lenses	1887	Eugen Frick (Switzerland)
Coat hanger	1903	Albert J. Parkhouse (USA)
Ballpoint pen	1938	Ladislao Biro (Hungary)

Most inventive

Thomas Edison was the busiest inventor ever. By the time he died in 1931, he had invented over 1,300 objects, about 15 for each year he lived. He invented the electric light bulb, a type of record player and the kinetoscope, the ancestor of the modern cinema. He also worked on an idea to use the human voice to power various machines, such as sewing machines.

DID YOU KNOW?

Scientists at the University of Western Australia have invented an amazing robot for shearing sheep. It has a long arm, with cutters at the end. To follow the shape of the sheep's body, the robot has to make one million calculations a second.

Chicle chewing

Chewing gum was invented by accident in the USA in the 1870s. Thomas Adams was trying to make rubber out of chicle, the dried sap of a Mexican tree. His son, though, enjoyed chewing the chicle. His father gave up his experiments and set up a chewing gum business instead.

Magic mold

In 1928, the Scottish scientist, Alexander Fleming, discovered that a type of mold could kill the germs that cause illnesses, such as pneumonia. The mold contained an ingredient called penicillin, an antibiotic drug. Today, doctors use penicillin and many other types of antibiotics to treat a very wide range of diseases.

Art and entertainment

Paint power

The Spanish artist, Pablo Picasso, produced a huge number of works in his long career. When he died in 1973, he had completed over 13,000 paintings. This is about 12 paintings for each month of his life. He had also worked on many thousands of engravings and book illustrations.

Beatle boom

The Beatles sold over 1,000 million records and tapes. This makes them the most successful pop group ever. Two members of the group, John Lennon and Paul McCartney, wrote more hit singles than anyone else. In the USA, 23 of their jointly-written songs reached Number One, and in the UK, 25.

DID YOU KNOW?

Perhaps one of the greatest musical feats was achieved by a Norwegian pop singer, Jan Teigan. In the 1978 Eurovision Song Contest, he scored no points at all for his song, *Mile after Mile!*

Blind poet

The English poet, John Milton, had to dictate his masterpiece, *Paradise Lost*, because he was blind. The work was published in 1667. Many people consider it the greatest epic poem ever written in English.

Making music

Wolfgang Amadeus Mozart started writing music when he was just five years old. By the time he died, aged only 35, Mozart had composed about a thousand pieces of music, including operas and symphonies. He wrote one opera, *La Clemenza di Tito* in an amazing 18 days.

Fooled again

Tom Keating fooled art lovers for over 25 years. He painted some 2,000 pictures – all of which were fakes. He copied pictures by Rembrandt, Renoir, Monet and other famous artists which many people mistook for the real thing. Keating always left a clue that his pictures were fakes, such as writing the word "fake" on the canvas before painting over it.

That's entertainment

Biggest painting	72,414 sq ft 6,727.5 sq m	Painted at Robb College, Australia.
Longest novel	Over 2 million words	*Les hommes de bonne volonté* by Jules Romain.
Shortest play	35 seconds	*Breath* by Samuel Beckett.
Longest-running play	15,000 performances by December 1988	*The Mousetrap* by Agatha Christie.
Largest musical instrument	33,112 pipes	Organ in Atlantic City, USA.
Longest film	15 hours, 21 minutes	*Berlin Alexanderplatz*

Amazing But True

One of the strangest sculptures was *Pont Neuf*, by Christo Javacheff. In 1985, he wrapped the Pont Neuf bridge, in Paris, in pink plastic sheeting. He used 440,000 sq ft (41,000 sq m) of plastic, enough to cover over 155 tennis courts.

Books for all

A British writer, Barbara Cartland, writes about 23 romantic novels a year. Some 500 million copies of her books have been sold around the world. These would make 850 stacks, each as high as Mount Everest.

Colossal Colossus

The Colossus of Rhodes was a huge, bronze sculpture of the Greek god, Helios. Built between 292-280BC, the statue was 117 ft (35m) tall. It stood astride the harbor entrance on the island of Rhodes. It was so big that ships sailed between its legs.

Silent world

Stagestruck

In 1899, the famous French actress, Sarah Bernhardt, played the part of Hamlet, although Shakespeare had written the role for a man. In 1915, Sarah Bernhardt had her leg amputated. She carried on acting and had parts specially written for her which she could act while sitting down.

Ludwig van Beethoven began losing his hearing when he was 30 years old. Despite this, he continued to compose many great pieces of music. By 1824, when his famous ninth symphony was first played in public, Beethoven had become completely deaf. He still helped to conduct the performance, though.

Animal antics

Railway baboon

In South Africa in the late 19th century, a chacma baboon called Jack earned his living as a railway signalman. In addition to his wages of 20 cents a day, he was also given half a bottle of beer on Saturdays.

Beetle power

For its size, the rhinoceros beetle is one of the strongest animals in the world. In a test, a beetle was able to carry 850 times its own weight on its back. This is like a person carrying ten African elephants on their back.

Locust destroyers

A large swarm of desert locusts can eat 22,000 tons of grain in one day. This is enough for everyone in France to have two cupfuls of grain each. The biggest swarm ever known contained 12.5 trillion locusts.

Pigeon hero

During World War II, the French army used pigeons to carry messages across battle lines. One of the pigeons killed in action was given the *Légion d'Honneur* medal. This is one of the highest awards for bravery.

Tortoise trial

In 1981, a tortoise in Kenya was sentenced to death for murder. People claimed it had killed six people, by magic. They were too frightened to execute the tortoise, though, and chained it to a tree instead. It was later set free.

Amazing But True

For its size, the tiny common flea can jump higher and longer than any other creature. It can do a long jump of about 13in (33cm). This is like a human jumping four soccer fields. A flea can also jump about 160 times its own height. This is equivalent to a human jumping to the top of the Eiffel Tower in Paris.

Rhino victory

In 1959, a rhinoceros called Cacareco was elected to the city council in Sao Paulo, Brazil. An astonishing 50,000 people voted for her as a protest against the high price of meat and beans. The election result was later disallowed, however.

Spider spinners

Spiders spin their webs with silk about 15 times finer than human hair. The silk is very light but can be stronger than steel. In Papua New Guinea, people use the webs of orb spiders as fishing nets. They are sturdy enough to hold a fish weighing 1 lb (0.41kg).

Homeward hound

In 1923, Bobbie, a collie dog, made a remarkable journey. He had been lost by his owners in Indiana. Six months later he appeared at their home in Oregon. He had tracked them 2,000 miles (3,200km) across four states, crossing the Rocky Mountains in the middle of winter.

DID YOU KNOW?

Termites are only about the size of grains of rice and totally blind. Yet they are master builders. Australian termites build huge, towering nests out of mud and saliva. The nests can be 20ft (6m) tall and 100ft (30m) wide. If termites were the size of human beings, their nests would be four times higher than the Empire State Building and 2.5 miles (4km) across.

Snake snacks

Some snakes can swallow animals as big as antelopes in just one mouthful. They wrap their coils around their prey, squeeze it to death and swallow it whole. One meal, though, lasts a snake a long time. In an experiment, a pit viper went without food for just over three years. It lost 61 per cent of its weight, but strangely grew longer.

Travelling animals

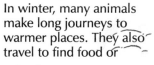

In winter, many animals make long journeys to warmer places. They also travel to find food or good breeding grounds. This list shows some of the most amazing of these animal travellers:

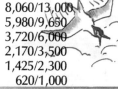

Animal	Distance travelled (one way) in miles/km
Arctic tern	12,400/20,000
White stork	8,060/13,000
Grey whale	5,980/9,650
European eel	3,720/6,000
Monarch butterfly	2,170/3,500
Noctule bat	1,425/2,300
Caribou	620/1,000

Amazing people

Rule of thumb

Shridhar Chillal of India has not cut his fingernails since 1952, despite the fact that his left thumb-nail alone measures 40in (101cm). This is nearly twice as long as an arm. The total length of the nails on his left hand is nearly 14.5ft (4.4m).

Mother love

A woman living in Russia in the 18th century had a grand total of 69 children. Most of the babies were born between 1725 and 1765. They included 16 pairs of twins, seven sets of triplets and four sets of quadruplets.

Channel escape

One of the first people to swim the English Channel may have been a French soldier, Jean-Marie Saletti. In 1815, he was being held prisoner in a ship near Dover in England. He is thought to have escaped by jumping overboard and swimming all the way to Boulogne in France. He must have swum at least 31 miles (50km).

Grand old age

In 1936, a Chinese newspaper falsely claimed that the world's oldest man had just died, aged 256. In fact, the chance of someone living past the age of 115 is one in 2.1 billion. The oldest person so far known was Shigechiyo Izumi from Japan. He died in 1986, at the age of 120 years and 237 days.

Amazing But True

Ferdinand Waldo Demara spent his whole life pretending to be someone else. He posed as a monk, a prison officer and a teacher. In 1952, despite having no medical knowledge at all, he was taken on as a surgeon in the Canadian Army. His first operation was a complete success. Eventually, a newspaper report about his success led to his exposure as a total fraud.

Whistling at work

The Mazateco Indians of Mexico do not need to use words to talk to each other. They can hold whole conversations just by whistling. They even buy and sell goods using whistles to give exact details about prices and quantities. The language is only used by men.

Wasp waists

In the 19th century, it was fashionable for women to have the tiniest waists possible. They achieved this by lacing themselves into very tight corsets. A French dancer, Polaire, had one of the smallest waists. It measured just 17in (42.5cm).

Medicine man

Samuel Jessop, a wealthy farmer, took medicines for all sorts of illnesses, although he never suffered from any of them. He took an amazing 200 pills a week and drank 40,000 bottles of medicine in his lifetime. Despite (or because of) this, he lived for 65 years.

DID YOU KNOW?

Roy C. Sullivan of the USA is the only person to have survived being struck by lightning seven times. He was struck for the first time in 1942, when he lost his big toe nail. In other strikes he lost his eyebrows and had his hair set on fire.

Human hail

In 1930, a German glider pilot survived falling to the ground in the middle of a gigantic hailstone. He and four others had bailed out of their aircraft over the Rhön mountains and fallen through a storm cloud. They were bounced up and down inside the cloud, and coated in layer upon layer of ice. The pilot who landed and survived had been cushioned by the ice around him. Sadly, the other pilots did not survive the fall.

On high

A monk, St. Simeon the Younger, spent the last 45 years of his life sitting on a stone pillar on the Hill of Wonders near Antioch, Syria. His strange lifestyle earned him the nickname "Stylites" from the Greek word for "pillar." He lived from about AD521-597.

Bed of nails

Indian holy men, or fakirs, sometimes test the power of their minds over their bodies by lying on beds of nails. They do not seem to feel any pain, even though the nails may be 6in (15cm) long. One fakir claimed to have lain on his spiky bed for an incredible 111 days.

Food feats

Monster meal

Josep Gruges made an enormous paella in 1987 in Spain. He used 4.1 tons of rice, 3.3 tons of meat, 1.6 tons of mussels, 1.5 tons of beans and peppers, 440lb (200kg) of garlic and 88 gal (400 liters) of oil. The paella was big enough to feed 40,000 people. They washed their monster meal down with about 8,000 bottles of champagne.

Big cheese

In 1964, a huge cheese was made for the World's Fair in New York. Nicknamed the "Golden Giant," it weighed 19.2 tons, as much as three African elephants. Some 184 tons of milk were used in the cheese, the amount produced in a day by 16,000 cows. The cheese was taken on tour in a refrigerated, glass "cheesemobile."

Meals on wheels

Gaston Menier invented an unusual way of serving his dinner guests in the 1880s. A railway brought the food from the kitchen to the table on top of carriages. These could travel at speeds of up to 2mph (3.2kph).

Stuffed camels

Bedouins make amazing dishes for feast days. They stuff fish with eggs, then stuff these into chickens. These are stuffed into a roast sheep and then into a whole cooked camel.

Wine waiter

In 1989, a bottle of red wine was on display in New York before being sold. It dated from 1784 and was worth over $480,000 (£300,000). Unfortunately, a waiter dropped his tray on the bottle and smashed it.

Top ten tea drinkers

Country	Cups per person per year
Great Britain	1,355
Ireland	1,302
New Zealand	889
Turkey	651
Australia	642
Sri Lanka	638
Egypt	576
Chile	427
Kenya	356
USSR	326

Animal appetite

Frank Buckland, a 19th century surgeon and naturalist, had very unusual eating habits. He would serve guests anything from crocodile to slug soup, mouse on toast, rhinoceros pie and whole roast ostrich. His worst recipes were for stewed mole and bluebottles. Even he could not eat them.

Amazing But True

The Ethiopian ruler, Emperor Menelik II, always ate a few pages of the Bible if he was feeling ill. He claimed it made him feel better. To help him recover from a serious illness in 1913, he ate the whole Book of Kings, page by page. He died, however, a few days later.

Calorie counters

Calories measure the amount of energy in foods. Adults need to take in between 2,500-3,000 calories a day. In some countries, though, people eat far more calories than they need.

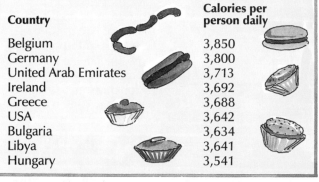

Country	Calories per person daily
Belgium	3,850
Germany	3,800
United Arab Emirates	3,713
Ireland	3,692
Greece	3,688
USA	3,642
Bulgaria	3,634
Libya	3,641
Hungary	3,541

Bear breakfast

In July 1969, heavy rain flooded the moat around the bears' enclosure in Brookfield Zoo, Chicago. The bears swam across the moat and escaped from their run. They made straight for a snack bar nearby. When their keepers found them next morning, they were happily feasting on a meal of ice cream and marshmallows.

Metal meals

A Frenchman, Michel Lotito, eats about 2lb (900g) of metal a day. Since 1966, he has munched his way through several bicycles, shopping carts and television sets, together with cutlery and razor blades. He has also eaten a whole light aircraft, which took him two years to finish. It takes him over 4 days to chew through a shopping cart.

Mind benders

Moving will

In the 1940s, a young girl in the USSR amazed scientists by turning lights on and off using her willpower alone. In a test, an egg was broken into a tank of water. By concentrating hard, the girl separated the yolk from the white.

Spoon bending

Uri Geller became famous in the 1970s for bending spoons and forks simply by stroking them or concentrating on them. He could even make broken watches work again, without seeing or touching them. Some people doubted his powers, saying he was just a clever conjurer.

Telling the future

In 1555, Nostradamus published his famous predictions about the future. Many of these have proved accurate. Nostradamus predicted the Great Fire of London in 1666, and the coming of Napoleon and Hitler. He made his predictions by looking into a bowl of water balanced on a brass tripod.

DID YOU KNOW?

Some attempts at predicting the future go hopelessly wrong. One of the worst predictions was made by a German astrologer, Johann Stoffler. He forecast a terrible flood in February 1524. People panicked and even built boats so they could sail away and escape. But the day came and nothing happened.

Human calculators

Some people can make extremely complicated calculations in their heads, without writing anything down. Thomas Fuller was a slave in Virginia in the 1700s. He could not read or write but it took him just 1½ minutes to work out how many seconds there were in 70 years and 17.5 days.

Amazing memories

Long before stories and poems were written down, storytellers and musicians memorized them so that they could retell or sing them. They must have had amazing memories. The *Mahabharata*, a famous Indian poem, was over 90,000 verses long.

Smooth talkers

The world's fastest talker is probably an American, called John Moschitta. He can talk at a speed of over 580 words a minute and still be clearly understood. An Indian, S. Jeyaraman, talked non-stop for 360 hours – a world record.

Record reader

A doctor in the USA can recognize long-playing records without playing them or even seeing their names. He identifies them by the grooves cut into the surface of the record. From these, he can tell exactly which instruments are playing and how fast or slow the music is.

Amazing But True

In the 1930s, a man called Kuda Bux became famous for seeing blindfold. He could even read books blindfold. In 1945, he rode his bicycle through heavy traffic in New York City without bumping into anything. No one knows how he managed to perform this feat.

Language master

Scientists have worked out that the most languages a person would be able to master at one time without getting too confused is about 20. A British broadcaster, George Campbell, went far beyond this limit. He used an amazing 54 languages in his work.

Out of thin air

An Indian holy man, Sai Baba, is reported to be able to make gold coins appear out of thin air and make fruit appear on trees. There are even stories of him bringing people back to life and restoring people's eyesight.

Ghostly dictation

There have been several stories of people claiming that dead writers or composers speak to them and ask them to write down their work. One woman in England has taken dictation from many famous authors. They include Charles Dickens and Jane Austen.

Feats of the past

Record reign

Pharaoh Pepi II of Egypt reigned for 94 years, longer than any other monarch. He came to the throne in about 2281BC, when he was just six years old. The shortest reign was probably that of Luis Filipe of Portugal in 1908. He had been fatally wounded and died just 20 minutes after becoming king.

Empire builder

The greatest empire ever known was created by Alexander the Great. He became King of Macedonia in 336BC and died in 323BC, aged just 32. In those 13 years, however, he conquered an area almost as big as the USA and nearly a third larger than the Roman Empire. It stretched from Greece in the west right across to India in the east.

Prehistoric painters

In 1940, four boys and their dog accidentally discovered some of the earliest paintings ever made. The 596 animal pictures, on the walls of the Lascaux caves in France, had survived for some 15,000 years, since the last Ice Age. Among the animals are horses, bulls and bison.

DID YOU KNOW?

In the 1940s, the island of Malta won a medal. The British king, George VI, awarded the island the George Cross, one of the highest awards for gallantry a civilian can win. It was given in appreciation of all the hardships the island and its people had suffered in World War II.

Shortest war

On 27 August 1896, troops from Britain and Zanzibar fought the shortest war ever. The Sultan of Zanzibar refused to surrender, so the British bombed his palace until he was forced to change his mind. The Sultan eventually gave in after the fighting had lasted for just 38 minutes.

Slave power

In 73BC, Spartacus, a poor slave, led a revolt against the Romans. He persuaded so many fellow slaves and gladiators to join him that, at one time, he commanded a force of some 90,000 men. Amazingly, Spartacus trained them to fight so well that they defeated two Roman armies. In 71BC, the slave army was defeated. The name of Spartacus, however, has always been remembered as a symbol of freedom.

The long march

In 1934, 90,000 Chinese communists, led by Mao Tse-Tung, set out to march an incredible 6,000 miles (9,650km). They were escaping from attack and persecution by the ruling nationalist party. It took them a year to march from Kiangsi to Shensi. They crossed six major rivers and 18 mountain ranges along the way. Only 22,000 marchers survived their ordeal.

Picture writing

The first people ever to write anything down were the Sumerians who lived in the area which is now Iraq. About 5,500 years ago, they invented a type of writing which used pictures, not letters, to represent words. They scratched the symbols on tablets of wet clay which then dried and hardened.

Amazing But True

King Mithridates VI of Asia Minor was so afraid of being assassinated that he made himself immune to poison. He took a small dose every day to build up his resistance. In 63BC he tried to commit suicide to avoid being captured by the Romans. But his experiment had been so successful that he could not poison himself and had to ask a slave to kill him with a sword instead.

Under siege

Towards the end of the 7th century BC, the town of Azotus in Israel survived for 29 years under siege before it surrendered. It was being besieged by a force of Egyptian soldiers, under the leadership of Pharaoh Psamtik I.

Boat bridge

In 480BC, the Persian king, Xerxes I, led his army to invade Greece. In order to cross the Hellespont, a wide channel of water, the Persians made a bridge out of boats. Their army was so huge that it is supposed to have taken seven days to march across the bridge.

Saving France

In 1429, a young peasant girl, Joan of Arc, led the French army to save the city of Orléans. It was being besieged by English troops during the Hundred Years' War. Joan said that God had spoken to her, telling her to go to battle. But Joan's enemies believed her to be a witch and she was burned at the stake in 1431. In 1920, however, she was made into a saint.

Legendary feats

Telling tales

There is a legend that there was once an Arabian king who killed every woman he married. His latest wife was a beautiful girl called Scheherezade. She found a cunning way of saving her life. Each night she started to tell her husband, the king, a story. But she always stopped just as the story reached its most exciting part. By keeping the rest of the story for the next day, and the king in suspense, she kept herself alive.

Gone fishing

Polynesian mythology tells how the god, Maui, created land for people to live on. He pulled up the islands in the Pacific Ocean from the sea with a fishing rod.

36

Sun struggle

The Aztecs believed that the Sun god was a brave warrior. Each night he fought against the powers of darkness so that the Sun could be reborn in the morning. He had to be kept strong, though, with offerings of human hearts and blood.

DID YOU KNOW?

In Greek mythology, King Midas was granted a wish by the god, Dionysus. He wished that everything he touched would turn to gold. His got his wish, but quickly began to regret it. As soon as he tried to eat anything, the food turned to gold. The king was soon starving. Even worse, he touched his daughter and turned her to gold too. He had to ask the god to take his gift back.

Moving mountains

The Hindu god, Krishna, once persuaded some herdsmen to worship Mount Govardhana, instead of the god Indra. Indra was furious and sent terrible rains down on them. Krishna lifted up the mountain on his little finger and held it above the herdsmen and their animals for shelter. After seven days and seven nights, even Indra admitted defeat.

Thor's feat

In Norse legend, a huge serpent lies in the sea around the world. It is so huge that it circles the world and holds its tail in its mouth. Thor, the thunder god, was out fishing with a giant. He hooked the serpent and, using all his strength, struggled to land it. But the giant cut Thor's line and the serpent was able to escape.

The twelve labors of Hercules

In Greek mythology, the hero, Hercules, is said to have performed these 12 tasks, all thought too dangerous or difficult for anyone to do.

1. He strangled the huge Nemean lion and used its skin as armor.
2. He killed the Hydra of Lerna, a monster with nine snake heads.
3. He captured the Ceryneian hind, a deer bigger than a bull, with bronze hooves and gold antlers.
4. He captured the ferocious Erymanthian boar.
5. He killed some of the man-eating birds of Lake Stymphalis and drove the rest away.
6. He diverted a river through the stables of King Augeias, to clean them out.
7. He captured the giant bull terrorizing Crete and carried it on his back to the mainland.
8. He captured the man-eating mares of King Diomedes and fed Diomedes to them.
9. He fought with the Amazons and killed their queen to obtain her magic golden girdle.
10. He killed Geryon, a monster with three heads, six arms and three bodies joined at the waist.
11. He stole the golden apples of Hesperides from a tree guarded by a dragon.
12. He went down into the Underworld to fetch the three-headed dog, Cerberus.

Pied piper

In 1284, Hamelin in Germany was plagued with rats. One day, a piper appeared and promised to get rid of the rats for a reward. The rats were bewitched by his music and were led out of the town and into the river where they all drowned. But the people refused to pay the piper. So he led the town's children away. They were never seen again.

Goose warning

In 387BC, Gaulish (French) warriors attacked the city of Rome. Some people escaped to the Capitol hill. When supplies ran low, they were tempted to eat the geese living in the nearby temple. It was lucky they did not. One night the geese saved their lives by cackling a warning of a surprise Gaulish attack.

Eternal life

The Sumerian king, Gilgamesh, was told that a plant growing at the bottom of the sea would give him eternal life. He attached heavy stones to his feet and dived down to the ocean floor where he found the plant. Unfortunately, on his way home, a snake ate the precious plant.

The giants' dance

According to legend, the stones used to build Stonehenge in England came from Africa. They were taken to Ireland by a race of giants and arranged in a circle, called the Giants' Dance. Years later, the magician, Merlin, used his magic to transport the stone circle to England.

Master builders

Strength in stone

Stonehenge, England, was begun nearly 5,000 years ago. The builders had no machines, or even wheels, to help them. They had to drag huge blocks of stone, each weighing as much as 13 hippos, from 25 miles (40km) away. The total hours worked by the builders of Stonehenge adds up to 30 million years.

Canal fever

The Panama Canal, which links the Pacific and Atlantic oceans, was built between 1904-1914. To build the 51 mile (82km) long canal, 43,000 men dug up enough soil to cover over 14,000 soccer fields. Many workers died from yellow fever and malaria and two whole years were spent clearing the swamps where disease-carrying mosquitoes bred.

Marble marvel

The Taj Mahal in India took 20,000 laborers 20 years to complete. It is made of white marble inlaid with precious stones. The Taj was built by Emperor Shah Jahan as a tomb for his wife. On its completion, the emperor had the architect's head cut off to keep him from designing a more beautiful building.

Amazing But True

The biggest structure ever built by living things is the Great Barrier Reef off the northeast coast of Australia. The coral reef is 1,260 miles (2,028km) long and almost 2.5 times the size of Austria. It was built, though, by tiny sea creatures, called coral polyps, which are less than 0.4in (1cm) long.

Roads for Romans

The Romans began building roads across their empire in about 312BC. By AD200 they had built about 53,000 miles (85,000km) of roads, enough to run twice around the world. The roads were so well built that some have lasted for over 2,000 years. Most modern roads last for less than 50 years.

Channel tunnel

In December 1990, French and British miners became the first people to walk between the two countries since the Ice Age, 19,000 years ago when the Channel was dry land. To bore the Channel Tunnel deep under the sea between Britain and France, enough chalky soil was dug up to make a medium-sized town.

Great engineers

Name	Country	Dates	Achievement
L. da Vinci	Italy	1452-1519	Canal lock gates
P. Tresaguet	France	c. 1750	First modern roads
Abraham Darby	Britain	1779	World's first iron bridge
John McAdam	Britain	1756-1836	"Tarmac" road surfacing
J. Finlay	USA	1801	Modern suspension bridge
Ferdinand de Lesseps	France	1805-1894	Suez Canal
Isambard Kingdom Brunel	Britain	1806-1859	Great Western Railway
Gustav Eiffel	France	1832-1923	Eiffel Tower, Paris
J. Monier	France	1867	Reinforced concrete

Volcano challenge

The 11th-century chapel of Saint-Michel-d'Aiguilhe stands on an ancient, extinct volcano near Le Puy, France. Its builders had to haul their materials and tools up to the top of the 260ft (79m) high cone in baskets.

At a gallop

The Tacoma Narrows Bridge in the USA was one of the worst ever engineering feats. In high winds, its deck swung up and down in giant waves.

The bridge was intended to withstand winds of 120mph (190kph). Four months after it opened, though, it collapsed in winds of 42mph (67kph).

Up, up in the air

Many of the steel frames for skyscrapers in the USA are put up by Mohawk Indians from Montreal, Canada. They walk across beams just wider than your foot, over 800ft (244m) above the ground.

DID YOU KNOW?

The Great Pyramid in Egypt was built over 4,500 years ago. It contains enough stone to build a wall 10ft (3m) high around France. Some 4,000 men worked for 30 years hauling 2,300,000 stone blocks into place. Each stone weighed up to 16.5 tons, about as much as 20 cars. The stone were pulled along on wooden sledges, using reed ropes.

Super structures

Steel appeal

The Eiffel Tower in Paris is 986ft (300.5m) high, as tall as 60 giraffes. It contains about 8,085 tons of valuable steel. In the 1920s, a con-man sold the tower for scrap. Luckily his plan was discovered, the deal called off and the tower saved.

Dam buster

The Itaipu Dam on the Parana River between Brazil and Paraguay is over 0.6 miles (1km) long and 620ft (189m) high. To build the dam, workers used enough concrete to make nearly five Great Pyramids.

Wonder wall

The Great Wall of China is about 2,150 miles (3,460km) long, with another 1,780 miles (2,860km) of branches. In total, it is nearly as long as the River Nile, the world's longest river. The wall was built in about 220BC. As many as a million workers died before the wall was finished.

DID YOU KNOW?

In 1740, the Empress of Russia gave a special present to a prince she disliked. She built him a new palace...out of ice. The bed and covers were carved from ice. Ice trees and statues stood in the garden. The prince was relieved when his freezing home melted in the spring.

Mammoth huts

People living 15,000 years ago in the Ukraine built their homes out of mammoth bones and tusks. They covered these with mammoth skins, moss and earth. One hut, found near Mezhirich, Ukraine, probably took two families a week to build.

Super tunnels

Name	Location	Length	Record
Seikan Rail Tunnel	Japan	33.46 miles/ 53.85km	Longest vehicular tunnel
Channel Tunnel	Britain/France	31.3 miles/ 50.4km	Longest international tunnel
St. Gothard Road Tunnel	Switzerland	10.14 miles/ 16.32km	Longest road tunnel
New York Delaware	USA	105 miles/ 168.9km	World's longest tunnel
Moscow Metro	Russia	19.1 miles/ 30.7km	Longest subway tunnel

Building bridges

Bridge	Location	Record
River Meles	Turkey	Oldest surviving; built c.850BC.
Humber Bridge	Britain	Longest single span 4,626ft. (1,410m).
Akashi-Kaikyo (due 1998)	Japan	Main span will be 5,839ft (1,780m).
New River Gorge	USA	Longest steel arch bridge 1,700ft (518m).
Huey P. Long	USA	Longest railway bridge 22,995ft (7,009m).
Sydney Harbour	Australia	Widest "long span" bridge 160ft (48.8m).
Royal Gorge	USA	Highest bridge; 1,053ft (321m), above the Arkansas River.

Light ahoy

The earliest lighthouse ever was the Pharos of Alexandria, Egypt. It was built in white marble in about 270BC and stood a full 400ft (122m) high, 52ft (16m) higher than the tallest modern lighthouse. A wood fire provided its light.

Digging deep

The biggest hole ever dug by human beings is a diamond mine at Kimberley, South Africa. The mine was open for 44 years. During this time, miners dug 25 million tons of rock. This would fill a line of wheelbarrows long enough to reach the Moon. They had only picks and shovels to work with.

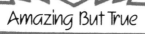

Amazing But True

In 1884, Sarah Winchester extended her house. She added doors which opened on to blank walls, staircases which led nowhere and a maze of rooms and windows. These were to confuse the ghosts she believed were haunting her.

Building big

The Vehicle Assembly Building at Cape Canaveral is the world's most spacious building. St. Peter's in Rome, the world's largest church, would fit inside it with plenty of room to spare. It was built in the 1960s to house the construction of the Saturn V moon rocket and the Apollo spacecraft. The doors alone are as tall as 70 men.

Rotten eggs

Two giant eggs, as high as five houses, have been built near Dortmund, Germany. Instead of resting on foundations, the eggs are being filled with water so they sink into the ground. In future, they will be used to process sewage.

Just for fun

Most on a motorbike

The most people ever to ride on a motorcycle at the same time is 46. These were members of a motorcycle club in New South Wales, Australia. They managed to ride for 1 mile (1.6km) on their 1,000cc motorbike.

Toy money

The board game Monopoly was invented in the 1930s by an unemployed heating engineer, Charles Darrow, from the USA. He had no idea how successful his idea would be. Monopoly is now the biggest-selling board game ever. By 1983, over 80 million sets had been sold. In 1975, twice as much Monopoly money was printed in the USA as real money.

Upside-down walking

In 1900, Johann Hurlinger of Austria walked the 868 miles (1,400km) from Vienna to Paris … on his hands. The journey took 55 days, with Hurlinger walking for ten hours each day. He travelled at an average speed of 1.5mph (2.5kph), half-normal walking speed.

DID YOU KNOW?

In 1988, a group of people in Alaska built the biggest snowman ever. It stood over 62ft (19m) high, taller than a six-story building. The snowman was named "Super Frosty." It took about two weeks to complete.

Eating out

An American, Fred E. Magel, claims to have eaten out some 46,000 times since 1928. He has eaten in restaurants in 60 countries all over the world. Lobster is one of his favorite dishes. Mr. Magel does not dine out just for pleasure, though. He works as a restaurant critic.

Puzzle solving

A woman living in Fiji took the longest time ever to solve the crossword puzzle in the British newspaper, *The Times*. In May 1966, she finished a crossword published 34 years earlier, in March 1932. In contrast, the fastest solver took just 3 minutes and 45 seconds.

Amazing But True

In the late 18th century, an English lord became famous in Paris for his odd behavior. He used to have dinner parties with dogs as guests. The dogs were dressed in fashionable clothes, with tiny shoes on their feet. The lord himself had thousands of shoes, as he would wear each pair only once.

Foot feats

In 1988, a Portuguese man, Antonio Gomes dos Santos, stood for just over 15 hours without moving a muscle. He set his record in a shopping center in Lisbon, Portugal. The record for balancing on one foot is 34 hours. It was set by an Indian, N. Ravi, in 1982.

All lies

For many years in the 19th century, Louis de Rougement fooled London scientists with reports of his time living with cannibals. He was exposed as a fraud only when he claimed he had cured himself of an illness by sleeping inside a dead buffalo. This did not stop him, though. He had great success with his one-man show, "The Greatest Liar on Earth."

Masked man

In 1908, Harry Bensley set out to walk around the world, as a bet. He had to wear an iron mask, push a baby carriage and make his living by selling postcards. No one was to see his face. By 1914, he had reached Italy and had just six countries to go. Sadly for him, World War I broke out and the bet was called off.

Losing bet

One of the worst horse racing bets was made by Horatio Bottomley in about 1913. To be sure of winning, he bought the six horses entered in a race. He told the jockeys which order to finish in and placed a bet on each horse to finish in a set place. Unfortunately, half way through the race, a thick mist came down and the horses finished in a terrible muddle. Mr Bottomley lost a fortune.

Dance marathon

In the 1930s, dance marathons were very popular forms of entertainment. There were also big prizes for the brave contestants. Two American dancers hold the record for the longest dance. They danced from 29 August 1930 to 1 April 1931, a total of 5,148 hours, 28.5 minutes. Their rest periods were gradually cut from 20 minutes to no minutes every hour.

Amazing feats map

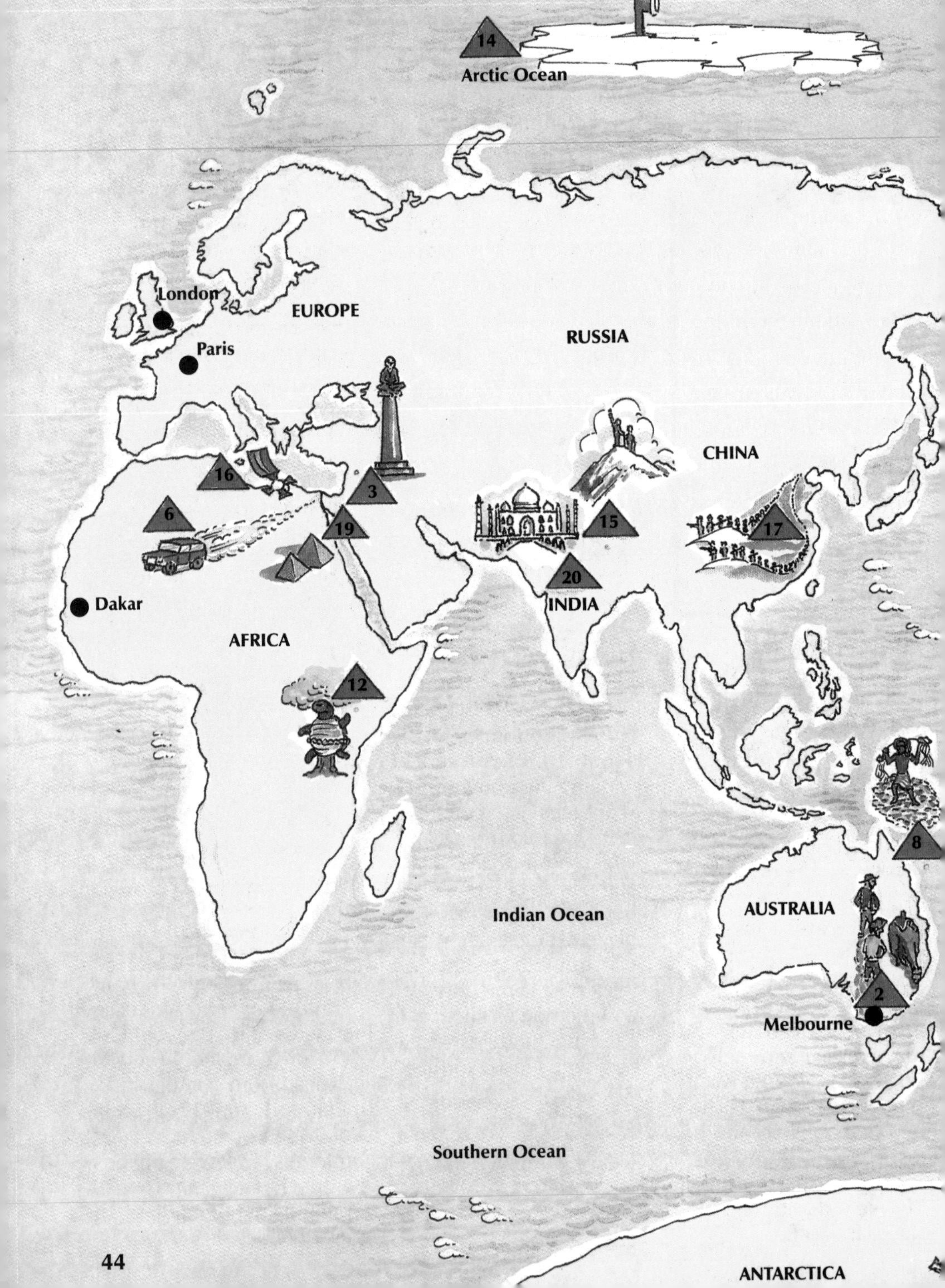

14 Arctic Ocean

London

Paris

EUROPE

RUSSIA

CHINA

Dakar

16

6

3

19

15

17

20

INDIA

AFRICA

12

Indian Ocean

AUSTRALIA

8

2

Melbourne

Southern Ocean

ANTARCTICA

44

CANADA

USA

New York

Pacific Ocean

Atlantic Ocean

SOUTH AMERICA

The numbered triangles show where some of the feats in this book happened. The feats themselves are listed over the page.

1 On 14 December 1911, Roald Amundsen and his four companions became the first people to reach the South Pole.

2 In 1861 Robert Burke and William Wills became the first people to walk across Australia from south to north, a journey of 1,488 miles (2,400km).

3 St. Simeon the Younger spent 45 years (AD552-597) sitting on top of a stone pillar near Antioch in Syria.

4 On 21 July 1969, Neil Armstrong became the first man to set foot on the Moon. He was part of the Apollo 11 Moon mission.

5 In May 1921, the American pilot, Charles Lindbergh, became the first person to fly solo across the Atlantic Ocean. He flew from London to New York.

6 The Paris-Dakar rally is the world's toughest motor race. Drivers have to travel almost 6,280 miles (11,000km), which includes driving across the baking hot Sahara Desert.

7 The CRAY-2 supercomputer is the most powerful computer in the world. It was built by Cray Research, Inc. in the USA.

8 In Fiji, priests walk over red-hot coals as part of religious ceremonies. Incredibly, they never seem to burn their feet.

9 On 30 June 1859, Blondin made his first crossing of Niagara Falls on a tightrope, stretched 1,100ft (335m) across the water.

10 Divers in Acapulco, Mexico, dive from a cliff 87.5ft (26.7m) above the sea to earn their living.

11 In 1959, a rhinoceros was elected to the city council of Sao Paulo, Brazil. The rhino received an amazing total of 50,000 votes.

12 In 1981, a tortoise in Kenya was sentenced to death for murdering six people by magic. However, it was later set free.

13 In 1895, Joshua Slocum set off from Boston to become the first person to sail solo around the world. His journey took three years.

14 In 1958, the US nuclear submarine, *Nautilus*, became the first vessel ever to cross the Arctic Ocean.

15 On 29 May 1953, Edmund Hillary and Sherpa Tenzing became the first people to climb Mount Everest, the world's highest mountain.

16 In the 1940s, the island of Malta won the George Cross medal from the British king. This is one of the highest awards for bravery.

17 In 1934, Mao Tse-Tung led 90,000 Chinese communists on a march of 6,000 miles (9,650km). Only 22,000 marchers survived.

18 In 1914, Ernest Shackleton and five companions sailed 800 miles (1,280km) in a small, open boat across the icy, stormy Southern Ocean to fetch help.

19 The Great Pyramid in Giza, Egypt was built in about 2,580BC. It took 4,000 men 30 years to haul 2,300,000 limestone blocks into place.

20 The Taj Mahal in Agra, India is built of white marble. It took 20,000 men about 20 years to complete. Work began in 1632.

Index

ISBN 0-590-22511-1

First published in Great Britain in 1992 by Usborne Publishing Ltd. Copyright © 1992 by Usborne Publishing Ltd. All rights reserved. Published by Scholastic Inc., 555 Broadway, New York, NY 10012, by arrangement with Usborne Publishing Ltd.

12 11 10 9 8 7 6 5 4 3 2   5 6 7 8 9/9 0/0

Printed in the U.S.A.
First Scholastic printing, February 1995